CANTICLE TO THE SUN

Most high, omnipotent, good Lord,
Praise, glory and honour and benediction all, are Thine.
To Thee alone do they belong, most High,
And there is no man fit to mention Thee.
Praise be to Thee, my Lord, with all Thy creatures,
Especially to my worshipful brother sun,
The which lights up the day, and through him dost Thou brightness give;
And beautiful is he and radiant with splendor great;
Of Thee, most High, signification gives.
Praised be my Lord, for sister moon and for the stars,
In heaven Thou has formed them clear and precious and fair.
Praised be my Lord for brother wind
And for the air and clouds and fair and every kind of weather,
By the which Thou givest to Thy creatures nourishment.
Praised be my Lord for sister water,
The which is greatly helpful and humble and precious and pure.
Praised be my Lord for brother fire,
By the which Thou lightest up the dark.
And fair is he and gay and mighty and strong.
Praised be my Lord for our sister, mother earth,
The which sustains and keeps us
And brings forth diverse fruits with grass and flowers bright.
Praised be my Lord for those who for Thy love forgive
And weakness bear tribulation.
Blessed those who shall in peace endure,
For by Thee, most High, shall they be crowned.
Praised be my Lord for our sister, the bodily death,
From the which no living man can flee.
Woe to them who die in mortal sin;
Blessed those who shall find themselves in Thy most holy will,
For the second death shall do them no ill.
Praise ye and bless ye my Lord, and give Him thanks,
And be subject unto Him with great humility.

In September 2003, I had the extraordinary experience of having three of my orchestral works recorded by the London Symphony Orchestra. During the sessions, I became acquainted with Timothy Jones, principal hornist of the orchestra. I have always loved the French horn, and Tim's virtuosic playing dazzled me. I decided then and there that I had to write a concerto for him, and happily he agreed.

Canticle to the Sun takes its creative impulse from the Protestant hymn tune most popularly known as "All Creatures of Our God and King." The tune, "Lasst uns Erfreuen" ("Let us Rejoice"), is found originally in the *Geistliche Kirchengesang*, dated 1623. The tune is built on a single musical motif of four notes and is extended by sequences and inversions.

Ralph Vaughan Williams harmonized the tune in 1906. The hymn sung by churchgoers today is based upon the text "Canticle to the Sun" written by St. Francis of Assisi, *ca. 1225*, and reflects St. Francis's pantheistic love of nature. The text was translated and adapted for hymn singing by William H. Draper in 1925:

All creatures of our God and King,
Lift up your voice and with us sing,
Alleluia! Alleluia!
Thou burning sun with golden beam,
Thou silver moon with softer gleam,
O praise Him! O praise Him!
Alleluia! Alleluia! Alleluia!

Thou rushing wind that art so strong,
Ye clouds that sail in Heaven along,
O praise Him! Alleluia!
Thou rushing morn in praise rejoice,
Ye lights of evening find a voice,
O praise Him! O praise Him!
Alleluia! Alleluia! Alleluia!

Thou flowing water pure and clear
Make music for Thy Lord to hear
Alleluia! Alleluia!
Thou fire so masterful and bright
That givest man both warmth and light,
O praise Him! O praise Him!
Alleluia! Alleluia! Alleluia!

All ye men of tender heart
Forgiving others take your part
O sing ye! Alleluia!
Ye who long pain and sorrow bear,
Praise God and on Him cast your care
O praise Him! O praise Him!
Alleluia! Alleluia! Alleluia!

Let all things their Creator bless
And worship Him in humbleness.
O praise Him! Alleluia!
Praise, praise the Father, praise the Son
And praise the Spirit, Three in One
O praise Him! O praise Him!
Alleluia! Alleluia! Alleluia!

Canticle to the Sun places the French horn soloist in the role of a celebrant, leading the players of the orchestra in a vibrant affirmation of beautiful melody, color, and texture. The work emerges from a sparkling string texture with the French horn weaving a lyrical strand of melody based upon the hymn tune. The work subsequently takes the form of a single-movement tapestry of fantasy variations based upon the simple triadic intervals and scale fragments of the hymn tune. *Canticle to the Sun* is intended as a showpiece for Timothy Jones's remarkable lyrical virtuosity on the French horn, and it was composed as a gift to him in celebration of his artistry.

Canticle to the Sun was composed from July 2004 through April 2005 in Norman, Oklahoma.

—Kenneth Fuchs

Kenneth Fuchs

Canticle to the Sun

Concerto for French Horn and Orchestra

PIANO REDUCTION

ISBN 978-1-4584-1912-5

EDWARD B.
MARKS MUSIC
COMPANY / HAL•LEONARD® CORPORATION

EXCLUSIVELY DISTRIBUTED BY

7777 W. BLUEMOUND RD. P.O. BOX 13819 MILWAUKEE, WI 53213

www.ebmarks.com
www.halleonard.com

for Timothy Jones
Principal Horn, London Symphony Orchestra

Canticle to the Sun

(Concerto for French Horn and Orchestra)

KENNETH FUCHS

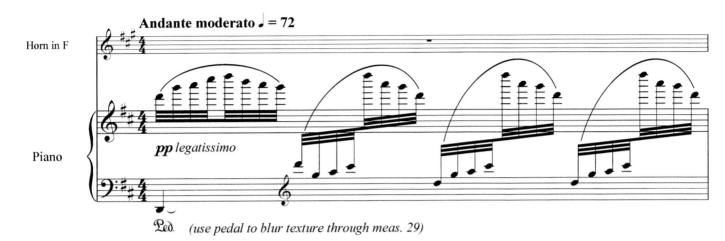

mp legato ed espr.

poco cresc.

(pp)

(pp)

p

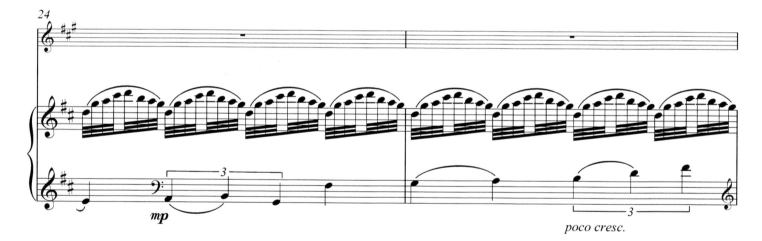

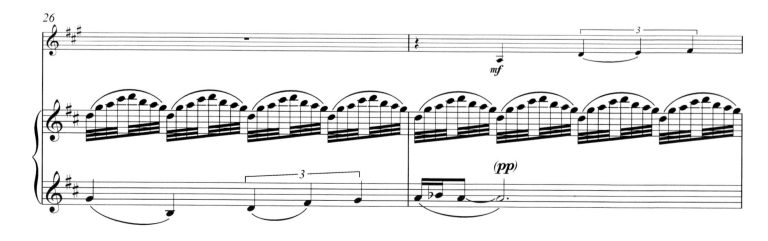

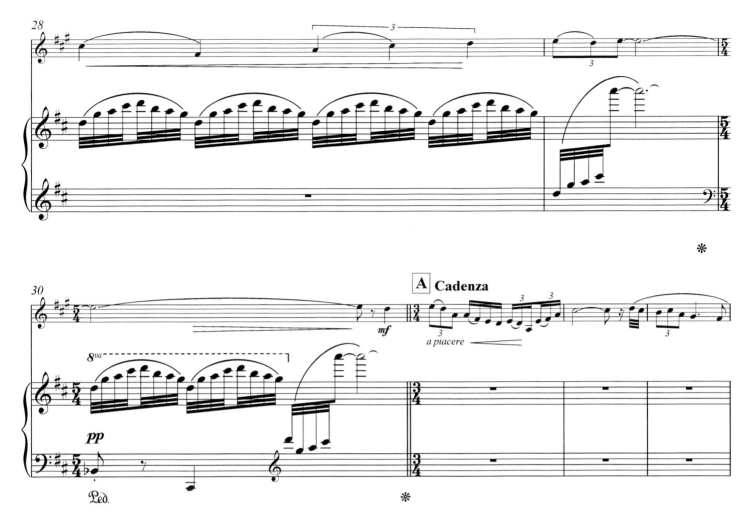

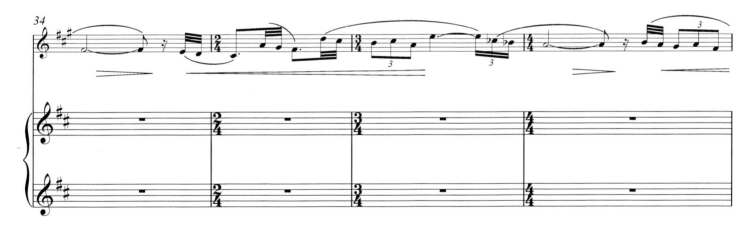

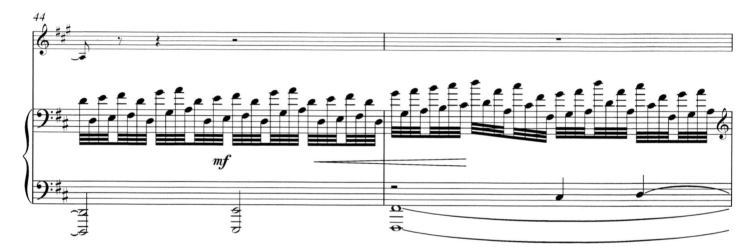

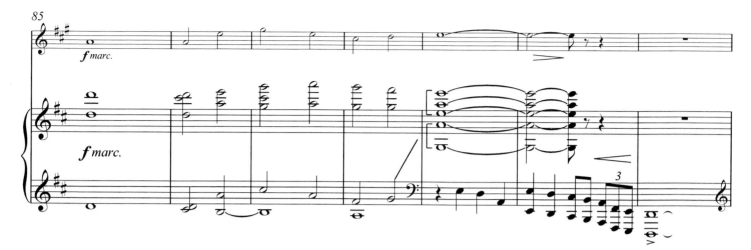

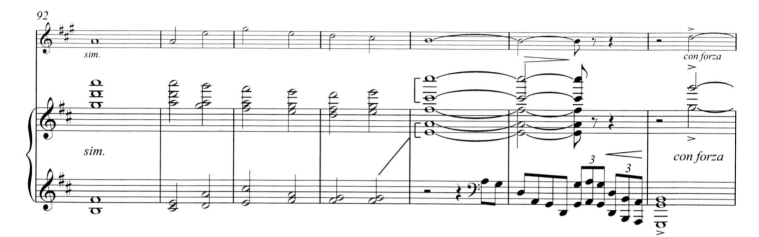

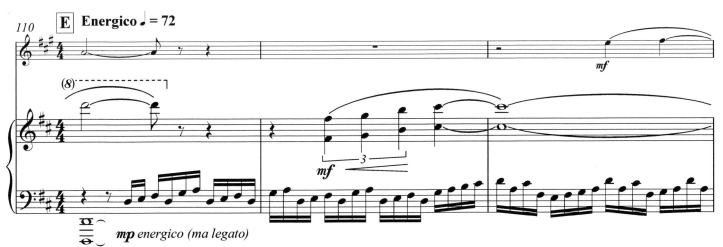

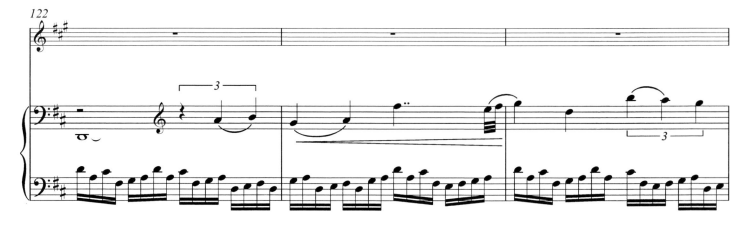

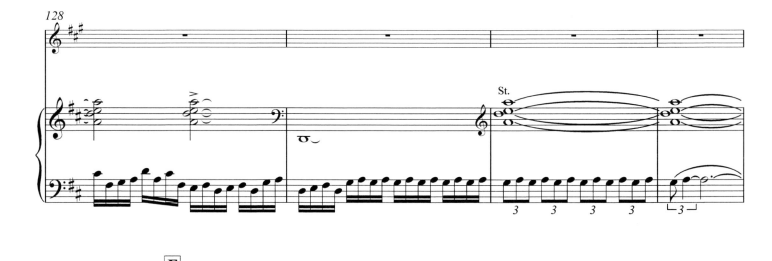

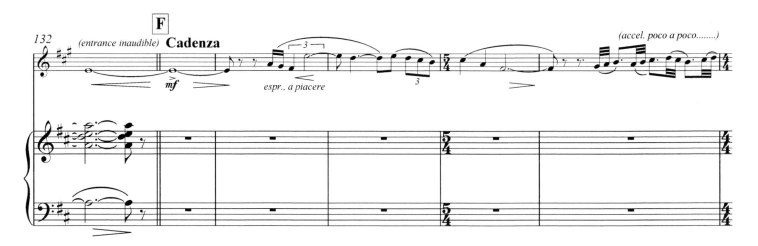

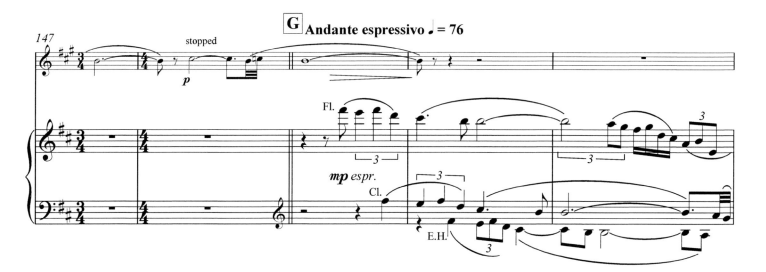

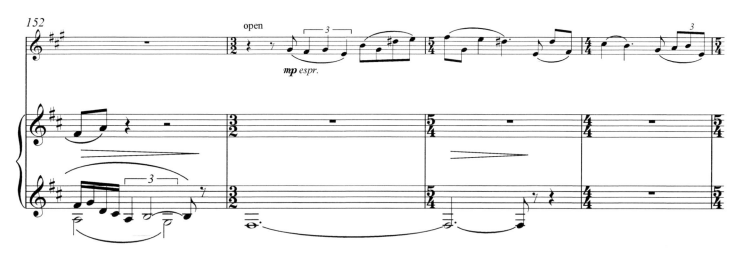

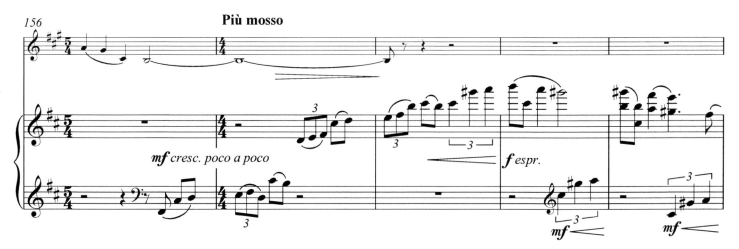

Kenneth Fuchs - Canticle to the Sun

Solo Horn in F

for Timothy Jones
Principal Horn, London Symphony Orchestra
Canticle to the Sun
(Concerto for French Horn and Orchestra)

KENNETH FUCHS

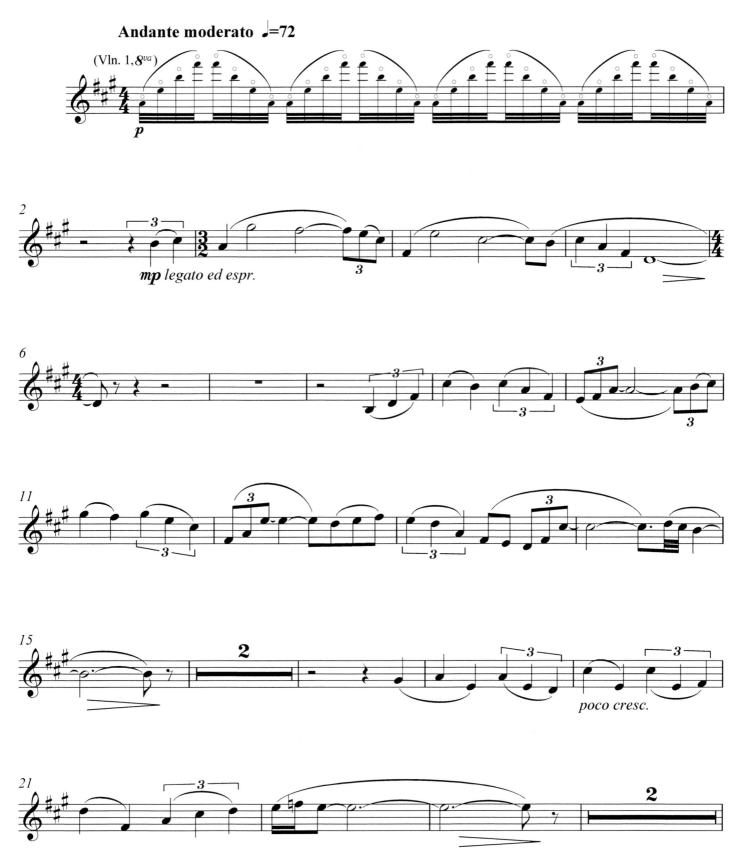

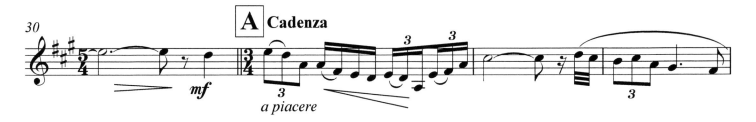

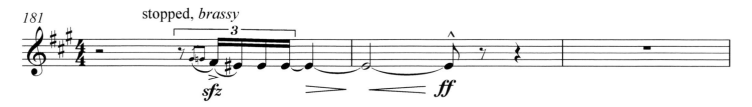

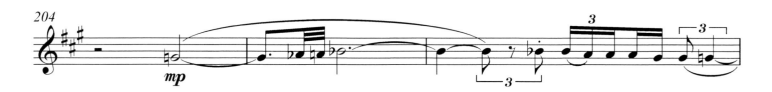

(V.S.)

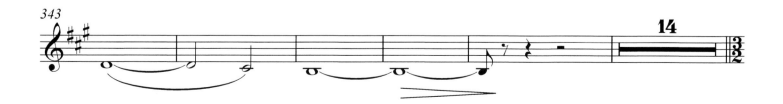

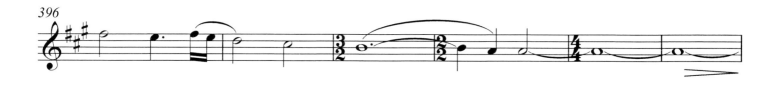

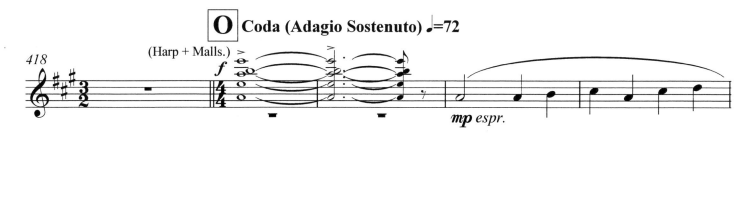

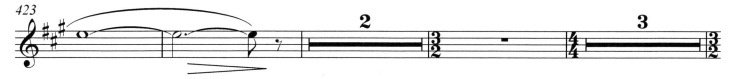

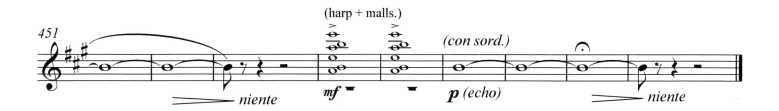

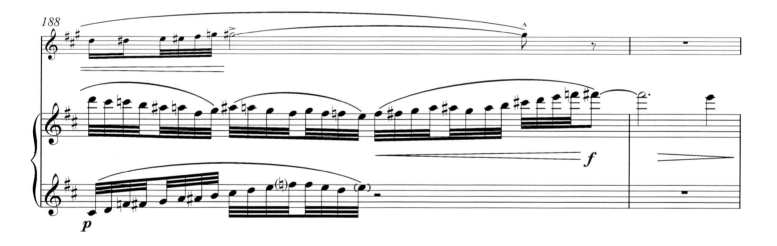

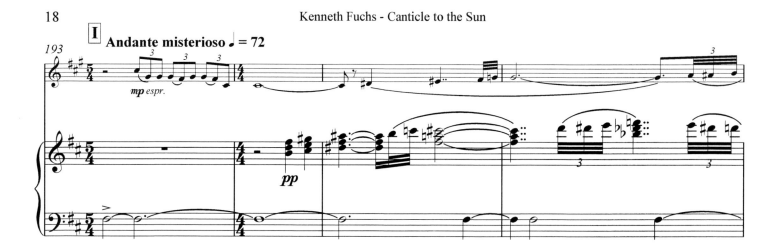

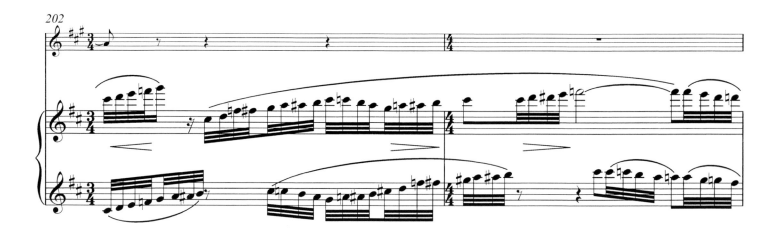

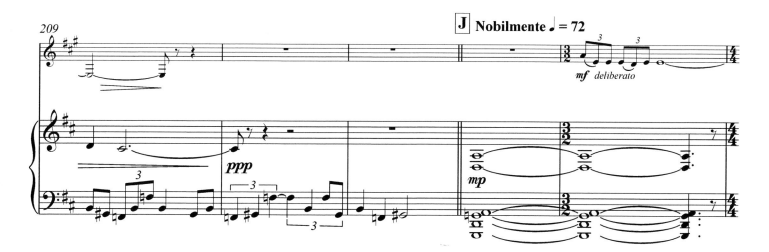

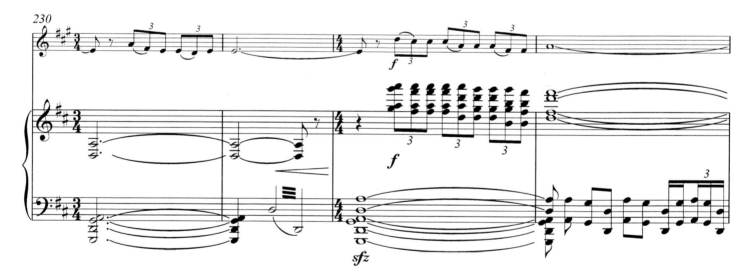

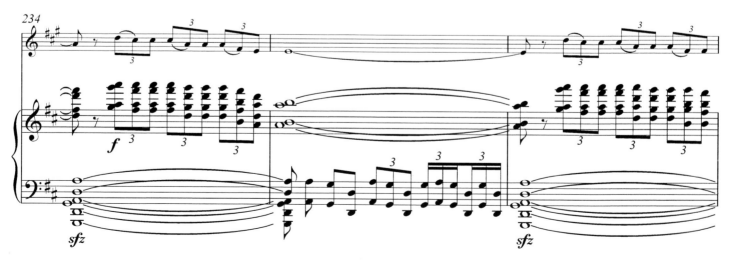

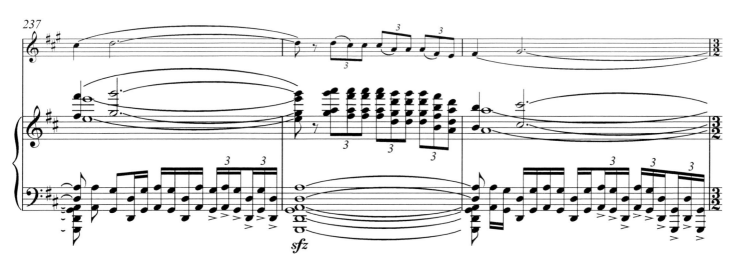

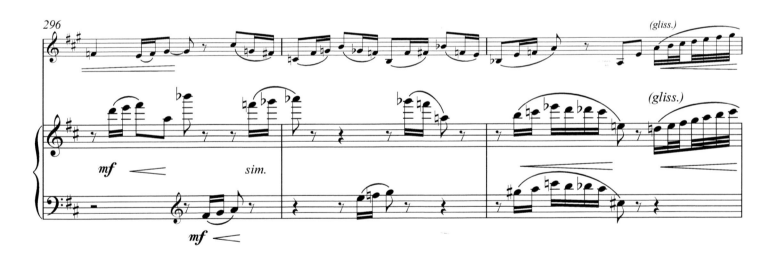

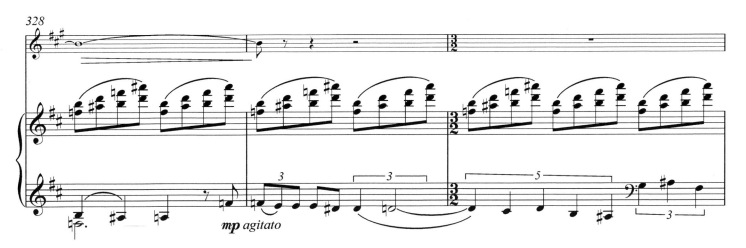

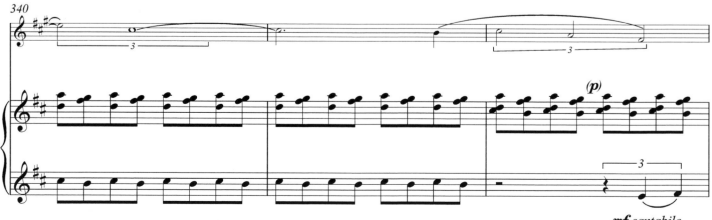

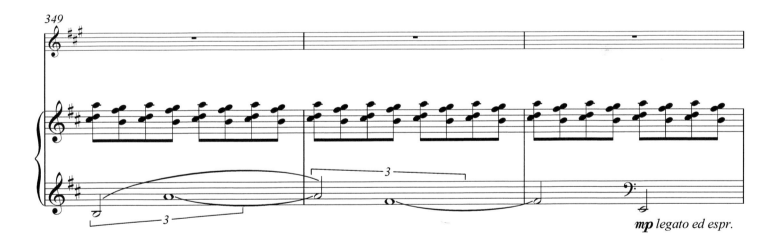

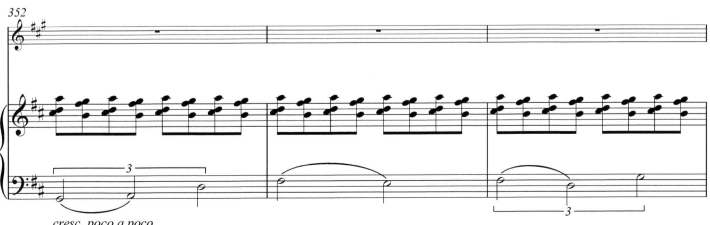

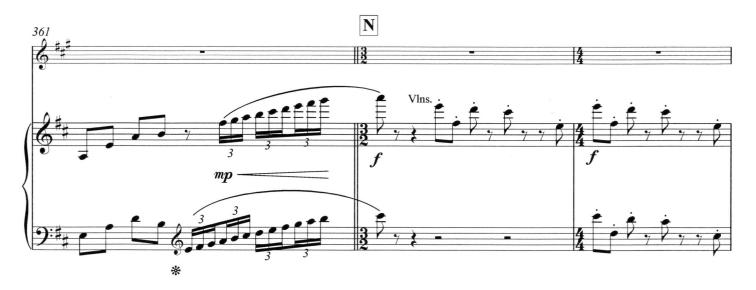

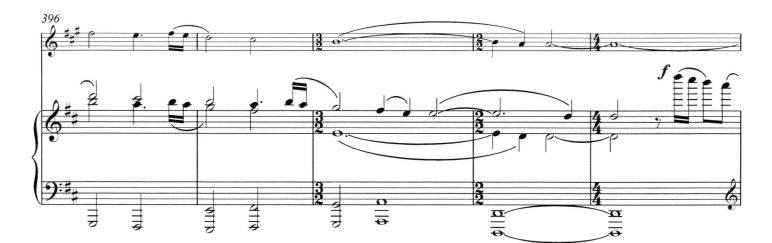

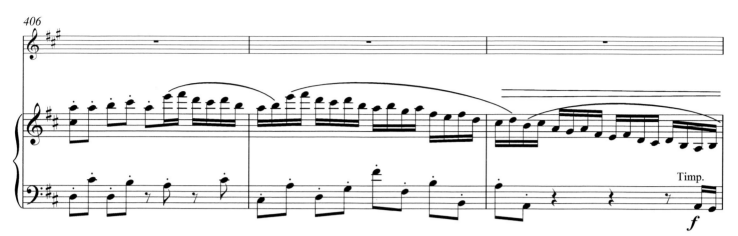

O **Coda (Adagio sostenuto)** ♩ = 72

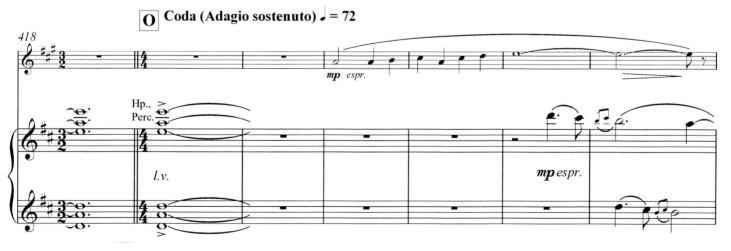

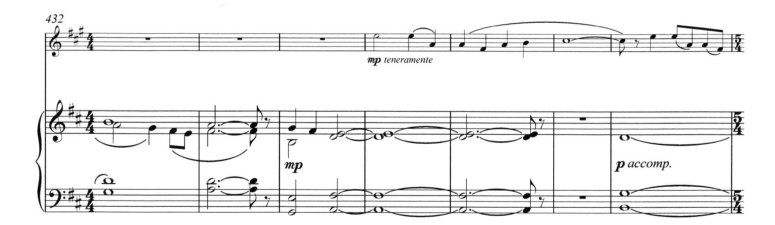

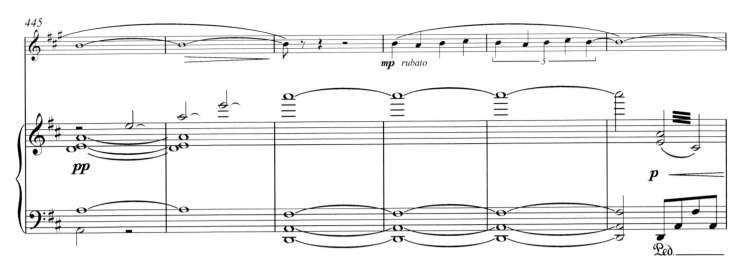

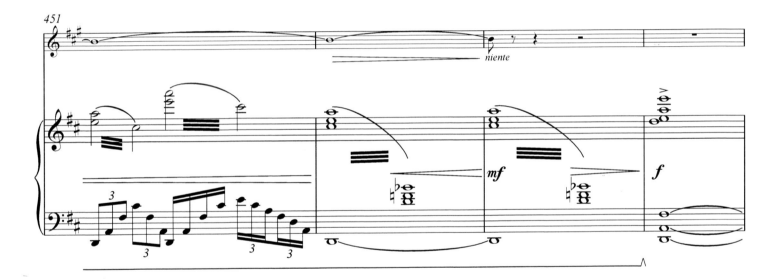

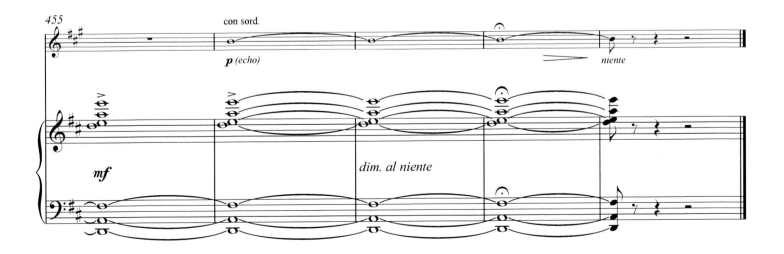